Picture book of

WALES

Castles, Stunning Scenery with Waterfalls, Mountains and Beautiful Coastline

Cardiff Castle

Llanrwst

Cardiff bay

Caernarfon Castle in Snowdonia

Snowdonia in Northen Wales

Aberystwyth

Pembrokeshire Coast

Snowdonia

Penllergaer Waterfalls Swansea

Swansea Marina

Cardiff bay

Cardiff Castle

Swansea

Aberystwyth

Snowdonia

Swansea Wharf

Monknash Beach in Glamorgan

Snowdonia

Aberystwyth

Tenby

Anglesey

Fall bay

Pembrokeshire

Snowdonia

Aberporth Ceredigion

Snowdonia

Pembrokeshire

St Davids Cathedral

Snowdonia

Portmeirion

Manai Bridge

Alwen reservoir

Portmeirion

Windmill on Anglesey

Cardiff bay

Monknash Beach

Cardiff

Caerphilly Castle

Printed in Great Britain
by Amazon